Charlotte
BRONTË

WHO WAS...

Charlotte
BRONTË

*The girl who turned her
life into a book*

KATE HUBBARD

✳ SHORT BOOKS

Published in 2004 by
Short Books
15 Highbury Terrace
London N5 1UP

10 9 8 7 6 5 4 3 2

A CIP catalogue record for this book
is available from the British Library.

ISBN 1-904095-80-1

inted in Great Britain by
kmarque, Croydon, Surrey.

MA	MB	MC
MD	ME	MF
MG	MH	MM
MN	MO	MR
AB	MT	MW

Chapter One

On the 10th August 1824, a day of bright sunshine and racing clouds, a small girl, holding her father's hand, stepped off a coach at Cowan Bridge in Lancashire. Behind her the coachman handed down a tin trunk, packed with three white and two flannel petticoats, one nankeen spencer (a short jacket), four brown and two white holland pinafores, two pairs of stays, day and night shifts, night caps, worsted stockings and two pairs of shoes. Such was the uniform of the Clergy Daughters' School. The new arrival was

Charlotte Brontë and she was eight years old.

As her father climbed back into the coach, Charlotte waved goodbye, knowing she would not see him or her home for an entire year. There was just one holiday, five weeks in the summer, and many girls spent that at school. Even letters weren't much comfort, as pupils were only allowed to write home every three months. She had left behind her beloved brother, Branwell, and her younger sisters, Emily and Anne. Although she looked forward to being reunited with her elder sisters, Maria and Elizabeth, who were already at the school, Charlotte found herself otherwise cut off from everything and everyone she loved.

Every detail of her first day at Cowan Bridge would remain etched on Charlotte's memory. She was shown to a large dormitory where the girls slept two to a bed. That night she found herself sharing with a young teacher, who snored like a wild pig, while Charlotte wept into her pillow. At six o'clock the next morning, a clanging bell propelled the girls out of their beds into a freezing room, where, with the help of a rushlight, they scrambled into their uniforms. Charlotte, bewildered and tear-stained, then followed them to the main hall, where, without having had a morsel of food, she had to stand for a whole hour and a half through morning prayers (regular doses of the Bible were the order of the day for pupils of the Clergy Daughters' School). Later, when she was presented with her bowl of porridge – horribly burned and containing unidentifiable foreign objects – she felt the vomit rise in her throat and her hunger vanished.

At nine o'clock, the other girls left for their first lesson. Charlotte was ordered to remain in the refectory, while a maid roughly chopped her long, reddish-brown hair (in accordance with school rules) to just below her ears. As she sat on her footstool, watching lengths of hair fall to the floor, her thoughts flew to home, the parsonage in the Yorkshire village of Howarth. Branwell, Emily and Anne would just be sitting down to lessons with their father. Her throat tightened.

In the next moment, she was brought up sharp by a summons from Miss Evans, the superintendent. It was time for her assessment, the test which all new girls at Cowan Bridge underwent on their first day.

'Welcome Charlotte,' said Miss Evans, as she beckoned Charlotte in. Her room, with its crimson tasselled tablecloth and brightly burning fire at least looked something like home. 'We do hope you'll be happy with us,' Miss Evans went on. 'We trust that you will apply yourself to your studies and always remember to say your prayers.'

'Yes Miss Evans,' replied Charlotte, nervously twisting the strings on her pinafore. Only then did she dare raise her eyes to the woman in front of her. Miss Evans was tall and stately, with her hair coiled over her ears. She looked stern, Charlotte thought, but not unkind, as she handed her some paper and a pencil.

An hour later, Miss Evans took Charlotte's work

from her, and dismissed her with a smile.

'You may join the others in the schoolroom,' she said, before noting down her verdict in the register:

Reads tolerably – Writes indifferently – Ciphers a little and works neatly – Knows nothing of Grammar, Geography, History or Accomplishments – Altogether clever for her age but knows nothing systematically. ('ciphering' meant arithmetic, and 'working' plain sewing).

Miss Evans could not possibly have known that her new pupil, barely three feet tall, peering shortsightedly at the paper, and so shy that her voice came out in a whisper, would grow up to become one of England's greatest writers, whose novels would enthral generations of schoolgirls.

***

The Clergy Daughters' School had been founded by

the Rev. Carus Wilson to educate the daughters of poor clergymen, in particular evangelical clergymen, of which Charlotte's father, the Rev. Patrick Brontë was one. For a mere £14 per year Mr Brontë could expect Charlotte to learn the skills and accomplishments that would equip her to become a governess (almost the only respectable profession for the daughter of a gentleman in 19th-century England). In Charlotte's day, there were about 50 pupils at the school. At eight she was one of the youngest (though her six-year-old sister Emily joined her in November), and while most pupils were between 8 and 14, there were some as old as 22.

The days at Cowan Bridge were long, hard, cold and, above all, hungry. After morning lessons, the girls had an hour of exercise in the garden before dinner. The menu was always the same – rice pudding to start (to fill empty stomachs) followed by meat and potatoes. But the globules of grey gristle and rancid fat, swimming in grease, looked like no meat the girls had ever seen.

The cook was known for her filthy habits – she thought nothing of picking up pieces of food from the floor and popping them into her dish; or of dipping her scab-ridden fingers into the pot, and then licking them. Several girls caught typhus fever from eating contaminated food – when the doctor was brought in to taste it, he spat it straight out in disgust – but it was only after some girls had actually died that the cook was dismissed.

After dinner there were more lessons and sewing, until five o'clock tea – half a slice of dry bread and a small cup of coffee – followed by a period of private study. Before bedtime prayers, the girls had a piece of oatcake, washed down with water. They went to bed with stomachs rumbling.

Sunday was the dreaded day of the week. Then, in addition to hours of Bible study, the girls had to put on cloaks and bonnets and walk two miles across the moors to the church, where Carus Wilson was vicar. In winter their shoes became soaked, while icy winds lacerated their cheeks. After listening to a two-hour sermon, they would eat a cold lunch, still sitting in the damp church, before embarking on the long walk home. As a reward – and not much of one – they were allowed a whole slice of bread with a thin scraping of butter for tea.

The regime at Cowan Bridge was actually no worse and a good deal better than other Victorian boarding schools, where inadequate food, filthy conditions, beating and bullying were rife. Boys' schools were especially bad – it wasn't uncommon to hear of boys sleeping eight to a bed on flea-infested mattresses. And children quite frequently died at school from the epidemics like cholera or scarlet fever that swept the countr in those days.

But for Charlotte life was quite bad enough. She was homesick, she resented being seen as a charity child (a poor clergyman's daughter) and, fastidious and private by nature, she recoiled from the rigours of boarding-school life. She was lucky, though, in being befriended by an older girl of 17 called Mellany Hane.

While Charlotte was clever but tiny, Mellany was a little slow-witted but built like an ox. When bigger girls tried to elbow Charlotte out of the way in the queue for dinner, or steal her piece of bread, her protector stepped in.

Charlotte's sister, Maria, was less fortunate. Maria was the eldest and cleverest of the Brontë children (at five years old she would read the newspaper aloud to her father). Charlotte worshipped her. But one of the teachers at Cowan Bridge, Miss Andrews, a sour-faced young woman with a mouth like a zip, picked on and persecuted Maria.

One day, while the girls were trying to warm themselves by the fire in the schoolroom, Miss Andrews yanked Maria by the ear.

'How dare you show yourself with dirty finger-nails, you filthy slattern,' she shrieked.

Maria made no attempt to defend herself, but Charlotte could not restrain her indignation.

'But Miss Andrews,' she burst out, 'the water in the pitcher was frozen this morning. Maria *couldn't* wash her hands.'

Charlotte was ignored and her sister meekly bowed her head while Miss Andrews took a bundle of birch twigs and lashed her bare neck. Charlotte seethed – how could Maria, so patient and good, be treated so unjustly? How could life be so unfair?

And Maria was unwell. She coughed continuously. Bright drops of blood spotted the handkerchief she held to her mouth. The skin on her face and hands looked ghostly and transparent. In an attempt to draw out her fever, a burning hot compress, known as a 'blister' was applied to her side. It was extremely painful (and quite futile), but Maria never uttered a word of complaint.

One morning she felt so weak that she couldn't get up. Miss Andrews dragged her from her bed and ordered her to get dressed. Again Charlotte remonstrated – 'Please Miss Andrews, Maria's ill, I think she needs a doctor' – in vain. With tears of anger pricking her eyes, she watched her sister struggle into her clothes. Downstairs Maria was punished by Miss Andrews for being late.

In February, Mr Brontë was finally told how ill his daughter was. When he arrived at Cowan Bridge, he instantly recognised the dreaded signs of consumption. He brought her back home, and nursed her tenderly, but three months later, at just 11 years old, she died. A message then came from the school informing the grieving father that his second daughter, ten-year-old Elizabeth, was also being sent home. Hours later, Mr Brontë watched helplessly as she was carried to the parsonage door, already far gone with consumption. The very next day, appalled at the thought of losing another child, he set off to Cowan Bridge to fetch Charlotte and Emily. They arrived just in time to say their goodbyes to Elizabeth, who within two weeks had followed her sister to an early grave.

Charlotte had spent a mere nine months at the Clergy Daughters' School, but those months shaped her view of the world – as a place of suffering and injustice – for the rest her life. She would always blame the school for the deaths of her adored sisters. Little did she know that their loss was just a foretaste of things to come.

Chapter Two

In the Brontës' day, Haworth, tucked into the Yorkshire moors, was a little-known, wind-blasted village, with one straggling, cobbled street. The wool trade provided some villagers with a livelihood, but for most life was a hard business. Every day long queues of people gathered to collect water, which was often green and stinking, from the only two public wells. As they stood in line, the wind, blowing straight off the moors, whipped around their ankles and whistled past their ears. But nowhere did the wind whip more keenly or whistle more loudly than around the last house in Haworth – the last bastion before the wilderness of the moors – the parsonage.

The Rev. Patrick Brontë, as the newly-appointed perpetual curate of Haworth, had moved into the parsonage in 1820, together with his wife Maria and their six children. With such a brood, Patrick and Maria had been relieved to leave their cramped old home, at Thornton, near Bradford, for a house with four bedrooms. The parsonage was certainly bigger than most houses in the village. It had the great and rare luxury of its own privy, and a two-seater (adult and child-sized) at that.

Stretching behind the house were the bleak and beautiful Yorkshire moors, so beloved by the Brontë children, while the side of the parsonage looked on to Haworth churchyard, jostling with gravestones leaning at odd angles as though beaten down by the wind. Scarcely a day went by without Mr Brontë conducting a funeral. The average age of death for Haworth villagers was just 25 years old, but all too often the coffin was little bigger than a shoe box. The sound of the funeral bells tolling, or the chink of the grave-digger's spade against stone, was background music for the Brontë children. They were no strangers to death.

One of Charlotte's very earliest memories, aged five, was of standing huddled with her sisters and brother at the foot of a big mahogany bed, where her mother, Maria Brontë, lay dying of cancer. Maria had come from a well-to-do Methodist family in Penzance, Cornwall, and was educated, devout, and as small as her husband was tall. She was devotedly nursed by Mr Brontë for seven long months. He tried every remedy, but to no avail. Maria's faith in God helped her face death calmly, but she could not feel the same about leaving her children motherless. The eldest, her namesake Maria, was only seven. During her last days, her pitiful cry – 'Oh God, my poor children, Oh God, my poor children!' – echoed throughout the house. She died on 15th September 1821.

After his wife's death, Mr Brontë asked her sister, Elizabeth Branwell – known as Aunt Branwell – to come and live at Haworth and help look after the children. Aunt Branwell found herself saying goodbye for ever to the warm breezes and golden sands of Penzance. She never got used to the bitter cold, the stone flags and curtainless windows of the parsonage.

Like her sister, she was an intelligent, well-read woman and she relished a lively, after-dinner debate about the issues of the day with Mr Brontë. She wore enormous bonnets, with a false hairpiece of curls protruding from the front, and she was very partial to snuff. Sometimes, as a tease, she would offer the children a pinch. They sometimes found her strict, and she never took their mother's place, but the children grew very fond of their aunt.

Completing the parsonage household were two servants, a cook called Tabitha Aykroyd, and a maid, Martha Brown. Martha was a girl of just 11, while Tabitha, known as 'Tabby', was a stout and quite elderly Yorkshire woman, who was very devoted to the 'childer', as she called them. Both stayed with the Brontës for the rest of their lives.

***

Relieved as she was to be home, Charlotte found the house silent and sombre. The trauma of her sisters' deaths was compounded by the fact that, from being the third child, she suddenly found herself promoted to the eldest, the one who the others looked up to, the one who was expected to be responsible. It was a burdensome and unwanted responsibility.

Nevertheless, she soon settled back into the familiar, never-wavering routine of parsonage life. The children's day began with prayers in their father's study, followed by a breakfast of porridge. They were all expected to do household chores – to make their beds and sweep the carpets (visitors remarked on how spotlessly clean the parsonage was) – before sitting down to lessons with their father.

After the tragedy of Cowan Bridge, Mr Brontë felt he had little choice but to teach his children himself. There were no local day schools. And, for girls in the 19th century, education of any kind was limited. Wealthy parents would employ a governess to teach their darlings the accomplishments proper for a young lady, whilst the poor had to accept that their daughters would remain illiterate and ignorant.

Patrick Brontë had had a far from easy start himself. He came from a poor family in Ireland, but purely thanks to his own talents and determination he had managed to win a place at Cambridge University and then to become a clergyman. When he wasn't composing his sermons he liked to write poetry.

He was a tall, gangling man, with red hair that turned quite white at an early age and stood up all over his head. Some found him a fierce and alarming figure. He had a habit of sleeping with a pair of loaded pistols by his bed, which he would discharge out of his bedroom window every morning. Once, when Maria Brontë bought a dress, which he considered too fine and fancy for a clergyman's wife, he cut off the sleeves with a pair of shears. But, even though he did not find it easy bringing up the children on his own, he certainly loved them and, especially after losing the two eldest, he did all he could to cherish them.

The children had lunch – usually meat and vegetables, followed by rice pudding or custard – at two o'clock. In the afternoons taking the family dogs, they set off for a walk across the moors. Branwell led the way, Charlotte followed, holding Anne's hand, and Emily, who liked to walk alone, brought up the rear.

One warm September's day, as skylarks soared and the children were returning to the parsonage after picking bilberries, Emily, noticed a stray dog cowering by the path. It was emaciated and panting heavily. Emily, whose affinity with animals was always much greater than with her fellow human beings, was instantly stricken.

'This poor dog's dying of thirst, I'm taking it home,' she announced.

Charlotte felt she must intervene – 'On no account will you do such a thing Emily. There is no knowing what might be the matter with it.'

'It needs water,' came the stubborn reply and she coaxed the dog, holding out phantom biscuits, back to the parsonage.

There, in the kitchen, Emily put down a bowl of water, whereupon she was bitten hard in the arm.

'Let's hope it doesn't have rabies Emily,' said Charlotte – trying, and failing, to keep a note of smugness out of her voice. 'We should call the doctor.'

Ignoring her sister, Emily stalked to the fire. While Charlotte looked on in horror, she seized a red-hot iron and cauterised the wound herself. Not a murmur of pain escaped her lips as the acrid smell of burning flesh filled the room. Later, when the arm became infected, the doctor did indeed have to be called.

On most afternoons, after their walk, the girls reluctantly joined Aunt Branwell for sewing. In her airless room, they would sit hemming yards of calico, or making frills for petticoats (much though she disliked sewing, Charlotte learned to make extraordinarily neat, almost invisible stitches) and counting the minutes until they could collect their tea, of bread, butter and jam, from Tabby.

On Sundays, of course, there was church, where the children would sit in the family pew and listen as their father preached his sermon, timed – Mr Brontë laid his watch on the side of the pulpit – to last exactly one hour.

But in the evenings came the longed-for moment when the children were free to retreat to a tiny room over the hall, known as the 'children's study', and to do what they loved more than anything in the world – to write stories and poems. For this they divided into pairs. Red-haired Branwell was a year younger than Charlotte. He was a brilliant boy, clever and witty, and, like Charlotte, he had a great talent for drawing as well as writing. Together they invented a marvellous and fantastical imaginary world.

It all began with a set of 12 wooden soldiers, given to Branwell as a present. He and Charlotte turned these soldiers into characters, called the 'Young Men'. The 'Young Men' began to appear first in plays, and then in miniature magazines that the children made – just five and a half cm tall and three and a half cm wide. This meant using less paper, which was expensive, but more importantly it was a form of secret code – the magazines could not be read by adult eyes, such as those of Mr Brontë or Aunt Branwell, without the aid of a magnifying glass. Written with a quill pen in tiny print, then illustrated and sewn and bound into brown paper covers, they were full of tales of magic and mystery. Gradually, Charlotte and Branwell created a whole imaginary kingdom for the 'Young Men', known first as 'Glasstown', then 'Angria'. Angria was in Africa and it was populated by beauteous heroines and dashing heroes, like the Duke of Wellington, whom Charlotte idolised.

All four children wrote obsessively – Emily and Anne, who were as close as twins, made up stories about their own fantasy world called 'Gondal' – and the fact that their spelling and punctuation were atrocious didn't worry them in the least. This is Emily and Anne's entry in their diary for November 24th 1834 (written, by Emily, on a scrap of paper less than ten cm high):

We are going to have for Dinner Boiled Beef Turnips potato's and applepudding the Kitchin is in avery untidy state Anne and I have not Done our music exercise which consists of b majer Taby said on my putting a pen in her face Ya pitter pottering there instead of pilling a potate I answered O Dear, O Dear, O Dear I will derictly with that I get up, take a Knife and begin pilling.

You would hardly believe that Emily was 16 at the time, let alone that she, too, would grow up to become a famous author.

When the children weren't writing they were reading. They devoured newspapers and would read *Blackwood's Magazine* aloud to each other and learn of gossip about the royal family or expeditions into darkest Africa or Napoleon's latest exploits; and such titbits of news would find their way into their stories. Books could be borrowed from a circulating library, so they were able to read poetry by Milton and Byron and stories like *Aesop's Fables* and the *Arabian Nights*. But their noses weren't always in a book. There were toys and games, too. They liked putting on theatrical performances. They had a set of ninepins and wooden alphabet blocks. And for the girls there were dolls with heads made of wax and real human hair, a child's tea set and a child-sized iron.

Above all, the Brontë children were everything to each other. Having lost their mother and their elder sisters, they clung together. Rare was the knock on the parsonage door; no children came to play; there were no visits to the houses of friends; no invitations to parties. The children's world existed within the parsonage walls. And, attached though they were to their father and aunt and the servants, Martha and Tabby, the bonds between themselves surpassed all others.

Chapter Three

The years slipped past happily. Then, in 1830, Mr Brontë became very ill and nearly died, which made him think seriously about the future of his daughters and what would become of them after his death. In 19th-century England a young woman was expected to find a husband and the sooner the better. If, by the age of about 25, she had failed to do so, she was regarded as an old maid destined to spend the rest of her life quietly at home dependant on her parents.

Possessed of neither beauty nor fortune, the

Brontë sisters could not expect a queue of suitors. This greatly worried Mr Brontë, whose curate's income of £200 was hardly enough to support his daughters while he was alive and would cease on his death. If they didn't marry, they would have to earn their livings, and that meant becoming a governess.

For such a position the girls required qualifications – languages, music, drawing – that Mr Brontë and Aunt Branwell could not provide. So, in January 1831, when she was 14, Charlotte was sent, in a covered cart, to a school some 20 miles away, at Roe Head, where her godmother, Mrs Atkinson, had agreed to pay her fees.

This, happily, was a very different kind of place to the Clergy Daughters' School. It was small, with just ten boarders, and run by a Miss Wooler and her three spinster sisters. Miss Wooler was a kind and intelligent woman. There was plenty to eat – though, remembering the revolting lumps of fat served at the Clergy Daughters' School, Charlotte refused to eat meat – and the pupils were treated well.

Charlotte began by being miserably homesick. But, slowly, life at Roe Head came to seem less black. In May Branwell appeared out of the blue, having walked all the way from Haworth to see his sister. And, for the first time in her life, Charlotte made friends. Her two best friends, who would remain so for the rest of her life, were called Ellen Nussey and Mary Taylor. Years later, when Charlotte had become famous, they described how she looked when she arrived at Roe Head – she was extremely small, very short-sighted (her weak eyes weakened further by all the miniature writing) and had dry, frizzy, brown hair. She spoke with a strong Irish accent that she had picked up from her father, she wore odd, old-fashioned clothes and she seemed terribly nervous and shy. In fact she looked more like a little old woman than a 14-year-old girl and she was not remotely pretty.

Mary Taylor told Charlotte to her face that she

was downright ugly. But people had only to talk to her, as Ellen and Mary soon discovered, to be struck by her unusual intelligence, her mischievous, some-times caustic, sense of humour and her fervid, impassioned nature. This, along with a pair of re-markably penetrating eyes, full of light and shadow, is what they remembered.

For Charlotte, however, her lack of beauty was a great bitterness. How different might have been her lot, she mused, if she could have boasted a pink and white complexion, fat golden ringlets and a shapely figure. Later, she would fill her books with heroines, whose plain, insignificant exteriors conceal passionate hearts.

Charlotte's eyes were being opened to a world beyond Haworth. She spent weekends and holidays at the houses of her friends. The Nussey home was well-furnished and sedate, while that of the Taylors was shabby, and rowdy with argument. Ellen and Mary were very different characters and they appealed to different sides of Charlotte. Ellen was pious, conventional, a dutiful daughter and sister. Mary was bold, independent and adventurous. Not for her was living at home as a spinster. Charlotte wrote jokingly, but enviously, that Mary had 'made up her mind she cannot and will not be a governess, a teacher, a milliner, a bonnet-maker or a housemaid'.

Some years later, when she was a young woman, Mary left England and, sailed by herself to New Zealand, where she became a very prosperous shop-keeper. Charlotte on the other hand would always feel bound by duty – as did most Victorian women, be it to fathers or husbands – whilst yearning for freedom, above all the freedom to write.

But, if she had little time for writing at Roe Head, she did at least manage to tell stories. Charlotte loved all things spooky. At night in the dormitory she entertained the other girls with ghost stories. A tale about a sleepwalker was so terrifying that one girl began having palpitations, help had to be called for and smelling salts administered. In consequence,

Charlotte and her listeners were fined for 'late talking'. But mostly she was a model pupil. She was top of the class for the whole of her time at Roe Head and she won the silver medal for achievement three terms in a row.

In 1832, Charlotte returned to Haworth. She was now able to teach her sisters, 14-year-old Emily and 12-year-old Anne, and she set them lessons between nine and 12 every morning. She and Branwell were busy, too, with their Angria stories.

'I'm just going to write because I cannot help it,' said Charlotte. Every evening, at nine o'clock, after their father had said evening prayers, wound the grandfather clock and gone to bed, the children would light more candles and take up their pens.

A few years later, in 1835, Miss Wooler, the headmistress of the school at Roe Head, offered 19-year-old Charlotte a job as a teacher and Charlotte felt obliged to accept. This time life at Roe Head was a good deal less happy. She described her pupils as 'fat-headed oafs'; she felt like a prisoner;

she couldn't bear having no time to write her stories; she missed Angria and Branwell.

Becoming more and more depressed, she fancied that she was ill and that those she loved – her sister Anne and her friend Mary Taylor – had consumption, the disease that had killed her elder sisters. Emily joined her at Roe Head, but she became even more desperate than Charlotte, for, as Charlotte explained, 'Liberty was the breath of Emily's nostrils.' Quite unable to survive away from home, Emily was soon sent back to Haworth. And when Charlotte could bear it no longer she followed her.

Shortly after getting home, and to her great surprise, Charlotte received her first proposal of marriage. Not just one, in fact, but two. The first came from the brother of her friend Ellen. Henry Nussey was a curate and a thoroughly good, upstanding man, but not one Charlotte felt she could love. She wrote a tactful letter to Ellen explaining she could only marry a man she adored and for whom she would be willing to die, and she did not feel that way about Henry. To Henry she wrote pertinently – 'I am not the serious, grave, cool-headed individual you suppose; you would think me romantic and eccentric; you would say I was satirical and severe.'

Hot on the heels of this proposal came a second, and from another curate, a Mr Pryce. After spending just one day at the parsonage, he wrote to Charlotte asking her to marry him. Once again she refused. Poor Mr Pryce was not destined to find a wife, for six months later he was dead.

As for Charlotte, she was now convinced that she would never marry. 'I am certainly doomed to be an old maid,' she declared to Ellen. 'Never mind, I made up my mind to that fate ever since I was 12 years old.'

There remained the necessity of earning a living. She certainly could not look to her brother to support her. Having gone to Bradford to study as a portrait painter, Branwell had suddenly come home, without any explanation. Charlotte realised that he had become addicted to opium and drink, that her brilliant, handsome brother was ruining his life and slipping away from her.

Nor was Emily suited to employment. Since returning home from Roe Head, she had made herself indispensable as housekeeper at the parsonage. But, to everyone's surprise, gentle Anne, the baby of the family, suddenly announced that she had found a job as a governess.

Charlotte felt that she must do the same – although the governess existence was one she dreaded, and, in her heart, scorned as being beneath her. Was she not born to write rather than teach spoiled brats?

Chapter Four

In 1839, when she was 23 years old, Charlotte became a governess to the Sidgwick family, who lived at Stonegappe, near Skipton. Her pupils were Mathilda, aged six, and John, aged four, and they were very badly behaved indeed. When Charlotte tried to stop the children from playing in the stable yard, where they were not allowed, John's elder brother threw a stone that hit her on the forehead, leaving a deep gash. Mrs Sidgwick asked her how she had got her cut, but Charlotte said nothing, which at least made the Sidgwick children like her rather more.

She certainly didn't like them. She complained to Ellen Nussey that she had to 'wipe the children's smutty noses' and that she was expected to sit doing 'oceans of needlework'. She hated being treated like a servant and not as a person in her own right – 'I see now more clearly than I ever have before, that a private governess has no existence,' she wrote. When, at dinner one day, little John Sidgwick put his sticky hand in Charlotte's and said, 'I love you Miss Brontë,' his mother raised her eyebrows and exclaimed in scandalised tones, 'Love the governess, my dear!'

The Sidgwicks liked to have parties and these were torture for Charlotte. She would shrink into a corner of the drawing-room, as loud-voiced men in frock coats strolled past twirling their moustaches and smoking cigars, and women, with petticoats rustling and skirts as wide as galleons, gossiped and giggled. Their eyes would slide over the young girl in the dark dress. Charlotte might as well have been invisible. But, it must be said, that if Charlotte complained about the Sidgwicks, the Sidgwicks complained about Charlotte. Mrs Sidgwick said that her governess would often spend whole days in bed and that she was terribly touchy, taking offence at the slightest thing. After just three months Charlotte went home.

Determined to make the most of her freedom, she plotted a trip to the sea, which she had never seen, with Ellen. Mr Brontë and Aunt Branwell would not countenance such an idea. It was not thought suitable for two young ladies, even grown-up ones of 23, to go off gallivanting around the country on their own, without a chaperone. To Charlotte's great annoyance, they insisted that, if she did go, she and Ellen would have to stay with a family they knew who lived at a farm near the sea-side town of Bridlington. To get their first longed-for glimpse of the ocean, the girls had to walk three miles from the farm, until they reached the cliffs and could look out over the great rolling swell of the

North Sea. But for the last week of their holiday they succeeded in getting to Bridlington, where they installed themselves on their own in a guest house. For Charlotte it was a taste of independence. She wanted more.

On her return to Haworth, Charlotte found a new arrival in the shape of her father's latest curate, the Rev. William Weightman. William Weightman was handsome, clever and charming. He was also a flirt. On Valentine's Day he walked ten miles to post Valentines for Charlotte, Emily, Anne and Ellen, who had come to stay with Charlotte. None of the girls had ever had a Valentine from anyone. They opened them giggling with excitement and puzzled, at first, by the strange postmark, until William sauntered into the parsonage and asked, with a twinkle in his eye – 'Could it be that any of you young ladies have received a Valentine?'

Charlotte pretended to find him ridiculous. She invented a nickname for him, 'Miss Celia Amelia', which may have had something to do with the fact that William was inclined to be vain of his sideburns. But secretly she was rather partial to the attentions of a handsome man, and she looked forward to his visits. Anne's heart, too, would beat a little faster when William's voice was heard at the door. But if both sisters allowed themselves to dream occasionally of how very sweet the words 'May I present Mrs Weightman', might sound, they kept those dreams to themselves.

in March 1841, Charlotte, all too aware that a life of leisure, pleasure and flirting was not for her, found a new position, as governess with the White family. The Whites were an improvement on the Sidgwicks. The children were not such 'little devils' and, she reported that, to her surprise, the 'fat baby has got to know me and be fond of me – occasionally I suspect myself of growing rather fond of it'. She enjoyed talking to Mr White, and Mrs White was an extremely kind and generous employer, for which proud, prickly Charlotte gave her no credit. Recognising that anything was better than being at the beck and call of others, she hatched a plot, with Emily and Anne, to start a school of their own. Aunt Branwell offered to lend the necessary money.

Then a letter arrived for Charlotte, from her old friend Mary Taylor, who, with her sister Martha, was at a finishing school in Brussels. She described to Charlotte the wonders of the city – the elegant mansions, the cathedrals, the museums and galleries, and the tiny cups of grainy black coffee. She urged Charlotte to come and join her and Charlotte's heart leapt at the prospect. Here was a chance for adventure, for a world other than Yorkshire. Desperate to go, she gave her notice to the Whites and succeeded in persuading her father and Aunt Branwell that six months spent studying in Brussels would greatly improve her qualifications as a teacher and so benefit the new school. It was decided that Charlotte could go, as long as she was accompanied by Emily. Both girls would be sent to the Pensionnat Heger, to study French.

Chapter Five

On the 8th of February 1842 Charlotte and Emily, escorted by their father, left for Belgium. The journey was an adventure in itself. They caught a train – a new experience for the sisters – from Leeds to London, which took 11 hours. They spent three days in London, where again Charlotte had never been and where she insisted on cramming in as much sight-seeing as possible. They visited the National Gallery, the British Museum and St Paul's, before catching the boat to Ostend. The voyage lasted 14 hours, and for Charlotte, as the boat tossed on churning seas and all three Brontës were violently sick, it seemed interminable. But the minute she saw the medieval towers and spires of Brussels, rising out of the plain surrounding the city she forgot the horrors of the journey and her spirits soared. A new life awaited her.

The Pensionnat Heger was run by Monsieur and Madame Heger. Monsieur was 33 and a professor at a nearby boys' school, the Athénée Royal. He was well known in Brussels as being a most brilliant and inspiring teacher, the kind of teacher who is never forgotten by his pupils. He was also a devout Catholic and very devoted to his family. Madame Heger was a few years older than her husband. They had three children, and a fourth, a boy, was born soon after Charlotte's arrival.

Charlotte and Emily shared a dormitory with 12 other boarders, though their beds were curtained off, which gave them some privacy. It felt very peculiar to Charlotte to find herself, at the ripe old age of 26, a schoolgirl once more, surrounded by girls much younger than herself and all Catholic too. Everything – smells, tastes, speaking French all day long – seemed novel and strange. But Charlotte, for once, didn't feel homesick. There was too much to think about, too much to take in. Monsieur Heger for one.

Charlotte had never come across a man like him before. In one of her letters to Ellen, she described him as 'a little black ugly being'.

Constantin Heger had known tragedy – his first wife and child had died of cholera – and he was frequently irritable and morose. He was liable to fly off into a rage during a lesson, hurling rubbers and sarcastic remarks. But seconds later his black mood would lift, all would be sunshine and smiles and he would be reaching into his pockets for the sweets and cakes he kept there as rewards. His pupils valued his praise for the very fact that it came so rarely. And none more than Charlotte.

Monsieur and Madame Heger soon realised that

the Brontë girls were no ordinary pupils. They were allowed to do some teaching, in return for free board and lessons in French and German. Their first pupils were the five daughters of an Englishman living in Brussels, Dr Wheelwright, and the girls became lifelong friends of Charlotte's. Emily, as usual, failed to make friends. In fact she was unpopular and the other girls found her awkward and impossible to talk to.

Unlike Charlotte, who liked to observe the world around her, who enjoyed conversation as long as it was intelligent, Emily looked inwards. And she couldn't give a fig what others thought of her. Long after they had gone out of fashion she insisted on wearing dresses with leg-of-mutton sleeves which did nothing to flatter her ungainly figure (Emily was several inches taller than Charlotte). The Belgian girls, who eagerly followed the latest Paris fashions, were bemused. And Charlotte noted their sniggers. She knew that her sister's heart lay in Yorkshire, in the wildness of the moors, that she yearned to be back there.

Charlotte did not. She was happy and stimulated. Occasionally, she managed to leave the Pensionnat and explore. Sometimes there were fêtes and concerts. Once, Queen Victoria came to Brussels and Charlotte saw her, a stout little woman laughing her head off, ride past in a carriage. She delighted in having some independence from her family. And she enjoyed Monsieur Heger's lessons, for however short-tempered he might be, she had never had such a spell-binding teacher.

In the September of that first year in Brussels, Charlotte heard some tragic news. Back in Haworth William Weightman had died of cholera. He was 28 years old. In Brussels, just a month later, Mary Taylor's sister, Martha, succumbed to the same disease. And, as if two deaths weren't enough, a letter from Mr Brontë informed Charlotte that Aunt Branwell had died.

Aunt Branwell had looked after Charlotte since she was five years old. She had been less than a mother, but more than an aunt and Charlotte had grown very fond of her. She left each of her nieces £300, which was not a huge sum, but at least provided them with a little nest egg. Charlotte and Emily travelled back to Haworth, but arrived too late for the funeral.

They brought with them letters, for Mr Brontë, from Monsieur and Madame Heger, full of praise for both girls, and hoping that one of them would be allowed to return to the Pensionnat. This of course was what Charlotte desperately wanted. All her interests, all her hopes, now centred on her life in Brussels. The thought of remaining in the parsonage was unbearable.

Mr Brontë, however, could not be left alone. Anne was now living with a family, the Robinsons, as their governess, and after Branwell had lost his latest job – as a railway clerk – she had managed to have him appointed as tutor to the same family. Luckily, Emily was as desperate to stay in Haworth as Charlotte was to leave. With Emily willing to act as housekeeper and to look after their father, Charlotte was free.

Years later she confessed to Ellen – 'I returned to Brussels after aunt's death against my conscience, prompted by an irresistible impulse. I was punished for my selfish folly by a total withdrawal for more than two years of happiness and peace of mind.'

This time she made the journey alone, which she nearly had cause to regret when she found herself late at night at London Bridge trying to board the boat for Ostend and being jostled and argued over by the watermen. Arriving safely back in Brussels, she began her new job, as Mademoiselle Charlotte, English teacher, at £16 per year. But her former contentment eluded her and she began to feel lonely and isolated. She missed Emily and Mary Taylor, too, who had gone to Germany. She refused to have anything to do with the other teachers and, as usual, she despised her pupils. The Belgian girls, she claimed, were selfish, inferior and no better than animals. But the real reason for her unhappiness, the explanation of the 'irresistible impulse', was Monsieur Heger, or, rather, Charlotte's feelings for Monsieur Heger. One of Charlotte's new duties was to give Monsieur Heger English lessons. She grew to know him better, and to like his company. She found herself listening for his footstep and his voice. She basked in a warm glow when he praised an essay she'd written.

Monsieur Heger was very far from being a handsome man; he did not, for example, possess the perfect profile and chestnut curls of William Weightman, but he happened to be the cleverest and most interesting man Charlotte had ever met. In short, despite knowing all too well that he was married, she grew to love him.

And how did Monsieur Heger feel? In all his years of teaching, he had never come across a pupil like Charlotte. He admired her great intelligence and her gift for writing. As a mark of his interest he took to leaving books that he thought she might enjoy in her desk, sometimes accompanied by a little note. When she opened her desk, Charlotte's heart would flutter – perhaps these books were gifts of love, not simply thoughtful loans from teacher to pupil. She treasured them.

But never for a moment did it occur to Monsieur Heger that Charlotte might see him as anything other than a teacher, that she might love him. Madame, of course, understood all too well. With a woman's intuition, she guessed how Charlotte felt. She did not want to hurt Charlotte's feelings, but nor did she want any whiff of scandal to touch her school. So she put a stop to the English lessons Charlotte was giving Monsieur.

Charlotte pretended that she couldn't understand why Madame Heger seemed to dislike her and why she was treating her differently. She convinced herself that Madame was spying on her and turned her into a villain. The happy days at the Pensionnat Heger were no more. Charlotte grew increasingly wretched. There was no one she could talk to about how she felt; she could scarcely admit her feelings to herself, knowing them to be wrong.

Lonely as she was, she grew a good deal more so during the long summer holidays. While the pupils went home to their families, the other teachers visited friends and relatives and the Hegers left for the seaside, Charlotte was left alone in the school, with just one servant to look after her. She wandered through the cavernous classrooms with their rows of empty desks. She paced the long dormitory with its rows of empty beds. She went for long walks through the hot, dusty streets of Brussels, deserted except for the odd stray dog or shuffling old woman. Charlotte, with only the company of her own tormented feelings, thought she was going mad. So desperate did she become that one day she walked into a cathedral and, even though she was not a Catholic, entered a confessional box. She persuaded the priest to allow her to make a confession. She had to pour her heart out to somebody.

In the autumn, the Hegers returned and the

school term began. But Charlotte had already decided that she must leave the Pensionnat. She gave her notice. At first Monsieur Heger, unwilling to lose the best pupil, and teacher, he'd ever had, refused to accept her resignation. He persuaded her to stay. But not for long. At the end of 1843 Charlotte left Brussels. Monsieur Heger saw her go with regret; Madame with relief. As for Charlotte, she felt as though her heart were breaking.

Chapter Six

She arrived home to find her father rapidly losing his sight and looking alarmingly frail. She felt that her place was at his side and decided that rather than starting a school elsewhere, as had been originally planned, she would have the school in the parsonage itself. With Branwell and Anne still living with the Robinson family, five or six boarders could be accommodated in their rooms. Charlotte would teach and Emily would act as housekeeper.

A prospectus was drawn up for 'The Misses

Brontës' Establishment'. It offered Writing, Maths, Grammar, Needlework, History and Geography. German, French, Latin, Music and Drawing were extras. Each young lady had to provide sheets, towels and a spoon. However, not a single pupil applied, probably because Haworth was so remote and there were few wealthy parents nearby who could afford to educate their daughters. The plan for a school had to be abandoned.

With time on her hands Charlotte felt listless and unsettled and she devoted her energies to writing endless letters to Monsieur Heger. While not obviously love letters, they were full of passion and feeling. She would anxiously wait for Monsieur's replies, which became fewer and fewer and then stopped altogether. But she kept on writing.

'If my master withdraws his friendship from me entirely I shall be altogether without hope,' she wrote, despairingly. She convinced herself that Madame Heger was intercepting her letters.

Monsieur Heger, however, was not the only cause

of Charlotte's unhappiness. Branwell had fallen in love with Mrs Robinson, his employer's wife, who was 17 years older than him, and she, it seemed, had encouraged him. When this was discovered by Mr Robinson, Branwell was instantly dismissed and he returned to the parsonage in disgrace. Charlotte was deeply disappointed in her brother. Although she too had fallen in love with a married man, who was also her employer, she, unlike Branwell, had kept her feelings hidden. She had suffered silently; there had been no scandal.

Branwell began to drown his sorrows in drink; he passed his days in the Haworth tavern. Mrs Robinson was sending him sums of money, which he used to buy opium from the drug-shop. But when the news came that Mr Robinson had died, hope returned. Now he could marry his love.

His love, however, had other ideas and lost no time in becoming Lady Scott, the wife of Sir Edward Scott. Branwell immediately sunk into despair. He didn't eat for three days or sleep for four nights; he seemed to be wasting away before the eyes of his family. So worried was Mr Brontë that he made a bed for his son in his own room, where he could watch over him.

Having given up all ideas of a school, with some relief, Charlotte had been turning over a long-held, secret ambition. Why, she reasoned, could not she and her sisters make money from their writing?

One day, while hunting for some wool to darn a stocking, she stumbled upon a notebook of Emily's, filled with poems. Unable to resist, she read them and found herself amazed by their wild passion and longing. This seemed the opportunity she had been waiting for and she resolved the poems should be published. But first she had to overcome Emily's resistance.

Charlotte's sisters did not share her hunger for recognition; they were quite content to write for themselves and to dwell in obscurity. In the end, however, Charlotte got her way – it was decided that all three sisters (Branwell was not included) would put together a book of their poems. Emily and Anne insisted on one condition – the use of pseudonyms. Charlotte, Emily and Anne Brontë would be known as Currer, Ellis and Acton Bell. People would assume the authors were brothers; the Brontës' privacy would remain intact.

Charlotte, the driving force, found a publisher, who agreed, in return for payment, to publish the book. Dipping into Aunt Branwell's legacy, she sent off the considerable sum of £31 10s. In May 1846, a volume of *Poems* appeared, by Currer, Ellis and Acton Bell. It was 165 pages long, bound in green cloth and cost four shillings. Two copies were sold.

Charlotte was not in the least discouraged. She had seen her work in print and the critics had greatly admired the poems. She decided the sisters should try their luck with the novels that they had been working on. Every evening, after Mr Brontë had gone to bed, the three of them would walk around and around the dining-room table reading out and discussing their manuscripts.

By July these were considered finished, so Charlotte bundled up her own book *The Professor*, Emily's *Wuthering Heights*, and Anne's *Agnes Grey* (still under their pseudonyms) and sent the package off to Smith, Elder & Co., a London publisher. Emily and Anne's books were accepted; Charlotte's was not, although it was thought to have promise.

But Charlotte's head had been busy for some time with a new idea for a novel, which she now longed to embark on. Her chance came in August when she took her father, who was now practically blind, to Manchester for a cataract operation. This was performed, like most operations in the 19th century, without any anaesthetic. Charlotte was in the room, but had to turn her eyes away; only her father's white knuckles, as he gripped the arms of his chair, betrayed his pain.

During the long, sultry August days of Mr Brontë's convalescence (the operation was a success) in their red-brick Manchester boarding house,

Charlotte sat down to write her new book. She wrote without stopping for five weeks, in pencil, crouched over her small, square notebooks. Once she got home to Haworth she continued, snatching every spare moment and ignoring an attack of awful toothache that made her whole head feel as if it would explode.

Her new novel was called *Jane Eyre*. Its heroine, Jane, is an orphan – small, plain and unloved – who tells the story of how she is sent to a boarding school, where the girls are cruelly treated and her best friend dies. Despite much hardship and suffering, Jane survives. She grows up to become a governess at Thornfield Hall, an eerie, gothic mansion. Slowly, against her better judgment, she falls in love with her employer, the dark, brooding Mr Rochester, who asks her to marry him. But just as they are on the point of exchanging their vows, the revelation of a terrible secret makes Jane flee.

Charlotte was, of course, drawing on her own experience. All her anger and misery from the days at Cowan Bridge were poured into her description of Jane's school, Lowood – 'the unhealthy nature of the site; the quantity and quality of the children's food; the brackish, fetid water used in its preparation; the pupils' wretched clothing and accommodations...'

Charlotte's love for Monsieur Heger mirrors that of Jane for Mr Rochester. Jane feels the same agony at the moment of parting – 'The whole consciousness of my life lorn, my love lost, my hope quenched, my faith death-struck, swayed full and mighty above me in one sullen mass. The bitter hour cannot be described...'

For Charlotte, the writing of *Jane Eyre* was like a dam breaking, a release for her pent-up feelings, Jane became her voice. This is what gives the novel its extraordinary passion and intensity.

On the 24th August 1847 Charlotte sent *Jane Eyre* to Smith, Elder & Co. An employee of the firm reported that he had sat up all night reading it, whereupon George Smith, the young proprietor, also took her manuscript home. He sat down on a Sunday morning and later recalled that, after just a few pages, the hairs on the back of his neck started to prickle. He didn't leave his chair, he missed every meal and by the end of the day he had finished the book. He accepted it at once, offering Charlotte £100. She could not help feeling this was meagre remittance for a year's work, but she was in no position to argue.

On October 19th 1847, she held *Jane Eyre*, by Currer Bell, in three volumes, in her hand. It was the most thrilling moment of her life.

The critics instantly recognised her book as a masterpiece. 'The best novel of the season,' wrote one. 'All the serious novel writers of the day lose in comparison with Currer Bell,' said another. By December, all 2,500 copies were sold out (it was reprinted in January, and again in April). The time had come, Charlotte decided, to inform Mr Brontë, that he had a best-selling author for a daughter.

Finding him in his study, she held out a copy of *Jane Eyre*.

'Papa, I've been writing a book', she said.

'Have you my dear?' replied Mr Brontë, and carried on reading his newspaper.

'But Papa I want you to look at it,' insisted Charlotte.

Her father sighed and rubbed his eyes —'I can't be troubled to read a manuscript.'

'But Papa it is printed.'

Mr Brontë frowned – 'I hope you have not been involving yourself in any silly expense.'

His daughter flushed a little but her voice was firm – 'I think in fact I shall gain some money by it.' And with that she left him to read.

Later that day Mr Brontë invited his children to tea.

'Children', he declared, struggling to conceal his pride. 'Charlotte has been writing a book and I think it is a rather better one than I expected.'

***

In December Emily and Anne's books were published. Sales for their works were poor, compared to *Jane Eyre* – though *Wuthering Heights* was considered highly original, if immoral. But, by Christmas 1847, all three Brontës were published authors and all of London was gossiping about the Bells. Many suspected that only women could express themselves with such raw feeling, that Currer, Ellis and Acton were not brothers, but sisters. Some thought they were one and the same person, not three. This rankled with the sisters. In July 1848, Charlotte and Anne, without Emily, who refused to go, decided to travel to London to reveal their identities to their publishers.

They arrived in a state of high excitement at 65 Cornhill, the offices of Smith Elder & Co, where they were admitted into a gloomy room full of large, highly polished pieces of furniture and piles of dusty books. Charlotte asked to see Mr Smith, whereupon a figure appeared and said dubiously 'Did you wish to see me Ma'am?'

In a letter to her friend Mary Taylor, Charlotte described what happened next –

'Is it Mr Smith?' I said, looking up through my spectacles at a young, tall, gentlemanly man.

'It is.'

I then put his own letter into his hand directed to 'Currer Bell'. He looked at it – then at me – again – yet again – I laughed at his queer perplexity – a recognition took place – I gave my real name – 'Miss Brontë'.

George Smith could hardly believe that these two 'rather quaintly dressed little ladies', anxiously clutching their bags, were the mysterious Bells, but he assured them their secret was safe with him. That evening he escorted them to the opera. Beside the other ladies, decked in jewels and gorgeous crinolines, Charlotte, in her country clothes and glasses, felt a 'queer, quizzical-looking being'. Nevertheless it was a day of triumph; she had no inkling of the tragic events to come.

Chapter Seven

Consumption and the effects of drink were slowly killing Branwell. On the 24th of September, while his family stood around his bed, he died, aged 31. Branwell, who had as much talent as his sisters and could have made a name for himself as a writer or an artist, had thrown his life away. It was an awful loss for Charlotte, who had once been so close to him and who remembered the brilliant boy he had been rather than the dissolute shadow of a man that he became.

'There is such a bitterness of pity for his life and death,' she wrote to Ellen, 'such a yearning for the emptiness of his whole existence.' She became ill with grief and shock.

On the day of Branwell's funeral, the east winds blew and Emily caught cold. Her cold turned into a hacking cough, she had a pain in her chest and she found it hard to breathe. It was consumption. Emily, with characteristic obstinacy, refused to see a doctor, or to go to bed. Hardly able to stand, she insisted on feeding the dogs – her own, a great hairy mastiff called Keeper, and Anne's, a little spaniel called Flossy. She clung to life. But on December 19th she was forced to lie down on the sofa in the dining room and there she died. Her funeral procession was lead by Mr Brontë and the faithful Keeper, who came into the church and sat in the family pew. For days afterwards he sat outside Emily's room and howled.

Within weeks of Emily's death, Anne too became ill. Doctors were summoned and Anne patiently submitted to all kinds of painful and useless treatments – she was dosed with cod-liver oil, blisters were applied to her side. In vain. Anne, who had never asked for anything in her life, had one dying request: to die by the sea.

Accompanied by Charlotte and Ellen Nussey, she was carried to Scarborough. She asked Ellen to be a sister to Charlotte. She died, very bravely and calmly, on 28th May 1849. Charlotte buried her last sister in Scarborough and returned to Haworth alone.

'Papa has now me only, the weakest, puniest, least promising of his six children,' she wrote.

The parsonage was steeped in melancholy. The loss of his children had aged Mr Brontë and he was now a crotchety old man. He preferred to eat his meals alone. Charlotte could hardly bear to watch Keeper and Flossy as, with heads hanging, they walked from room to room in search of their mistresses. She smuggled them into her bed at night. She felt her loneliness and grief like a physical pain, an aching emptiness that never left her. In an attempt to distract herself, she started a new novel, *Shirley*.

'Work is my best companion' she declared.

Even now, only her father, George Smith and Mary Taylor, who was safely in New Zealand, knew the true identity of Currer Bell. But people had begun to suspect, and rumours flew. On one occasion, Ellen asked Charlotte outright, and received a curt denial (Charlotte could not forget her promise to her sisters). Friends speculated, neighbours gossiped, the Haworth stationer wondered what Miss Brontë was doing with such quantities of paper and it was just a matter of time before her secret was out.

'I no longer walk invisible,' said Charlotte. She found herself a celebrity.

Fans of *Jane Eyre* came knocking on the door of the parsonage; invitations arrived by every post. Most were unwelcome. She had no desire to go to the grand houses of local bigwigs, or to glittering parties. She did not, however, refuse an invitation to stay with George Smith and his mother, in London.

Charlotte's shyness did not make her the easiest of guests, but the Smiths did their best to entertain her. They took her to the theatre, to lectures, to an exhibition of Turner's paintings, to the zoo, to the latest attraction – the Great Exhibition, in Hyde Park – and, at her own request, to visit a prison.

George Smith became a very kind friend to Charlotte. They wrote to each other regularly and he sent her parcels of books. He invited her to Scotland, where she went, and to visit the Rhine, which she did not. He was handsome and good-natured and he may have been a little in love with her and she with him.

Ellen certainly thought that George Smith wanted to marry Charlotte and teased her about him, which annoyed her enormously. How, Charlotte reasoned, could the eligible George admire such a person as herself – so small and stunted, so crooked of mouth, so large of nose, so sallow of skin? It was impossible. George himself was well aware of Charlotte's sensitivity about her looks and believed 'that she would have given all her genius and fame to have been beautiful'.

London was agog to see the author of *Jane Eyre*. On 12th June 1850, William Makepeace Thackeray, one of the most famous writers of the day, invited Charlotte to dinner. Thackeray was a great hero of Charlotte's, while *Jane Eyre* had made him cry. Charlotte was so excited that she couldn't eat all day; Thackeray's daughters were just as excited by the prospect of meeting the great Charlotte Brontë.

The evening was not a success. Charlotte had bought, specially for the occasion, a hairpiece made of brown silk, which unfortunately failed to match her own hair. The minute she arrived and saw the roomful of fashionable society ladies, she realised that she looked ridiculous – as if she had a pin-cushion stuck on top of her head.

Retiring to a corner of the drawing-room, she began talking to the one person she felt comfortable with, the governess, Miss Truelock. She saw Thackeray approaching. Enormously tall, he loomed over Charlotte, shook her tiny hand, and, turning to the old lady at his side, said – 'Mother, you must allow me to introduce you to Jane Eyre.'

Charlotte was mortified. She drew herself up to her full height, still barely reaching Thackeray's elbow, and replied, her voice trembling with emotion – 'My name, Sir, is Charlotte Brontë.'

The two writers never became friends. Thackeray thought her prickly as a thicket of thorns – 'There's a fire raging in that little woman,' he wrote. He was right.

Another famous Victorian author, Mrs Gaskell, did become a firm friend. Charlotte felt that here was someone she could talk to, who made her feel at home. Mrs Gaskell later described Charlotte as 'very little and very plain', with several missing teeth and remarkable eyes. In the years that followed, Charlotte often went to stay with the Gaskells in Manchester, and even became very attached to their daughters.

For all Charlotte's lack of beauty, she did not lack admirers and in 1851 she received her third offer of marriage, from James Taylor, who worked for Smith, Elder & Co. He had fallen in love with Charlotte and started writing her letters. On April 4th, just before leaving for India, where he had been posted, he came to Haworth and made his proposal.

Charlotte refused him, and the disappointed Mr Taylor went to India, but he continued to write to her. When his letters eventually dried up Charlotte, perversely, found she missed them. She felt lonelier than ever. Battling against depression and bad health, she managed to write her fourth novel, *Villette*.

Chapter Eight

Charlotte's gloom, she explained, arose 'not because I am a single woman and likely to remain a single woman, but because I am a lonely woman and likely to remain lonely.'

In 1852, when Charlotte was 36, she was offered a chance to put both behind her. Arthur Bell Nicholls had arrived in Haworth in 1845, as Mr Brontë's new curate. Like Mr Brontë, he was an Irishman, with a big, square face and whiskers that almost reached to his chin. If a little stiff, he was a good man, popular with the people of Haworth and trusted by Mr Brontë. While Emily and Anne were dying, he had walked their dogs and shown himself to be a friend. For some time now, he had loved Charlotte from afar, although she had scarcely noticed him. As a rule she took a dim view of curates.

On December 13th Mr Nicholls came for tea with her father. Charlotte, sitting alone in the dining room, heard him say his goodbyes. Then there was a tap on the door, and he entered and stood before her, quivering from head to toe.

Without preamble, his voice shaking, he burst out with – 'Miss B-B-B Brontë – could you ever – would you – do me the honour of becoming my wife?'

Charlotte, dumbfounded, replied – 'I scarcely know what to say Mr Nicholls.'

'Can you at least give me leave to hope?' begged her hapless suitor. Charlotte was firm. 'I must speak to my father. You must allow me to give you an answer tomorrow,' and she showed him to the door.

Mr Brontë instantly flew into a rage – the veins stood out on his forehead, his eyes became bloodshot, he ranted and raved. As far as he was concerned, Mr Nicholls was a good enough curate, but not good enough for his daughter. He also, though he wouldn't admit it, hated the thought of loosing his only surviving child.

Knowing how her father felt, Charlotte refused Mr Nicholls, who promptly resigned. His suffering was terrible to see. And Charlotte understood; she knew the torment of loving someone and not being loved in return. She pitied him. On the day he was due to leave Haworth he came to say goodbye and Charlotte found him leaning against the garden door of the parsonage, his body shaking with sobs.

But Mr Nicholls was a determined man. He started writing to Charlotte and, after she had received six letters, she relented and began to reply to him, without telling her father. Then came the news that George Smith was to marry the beautiful daughter of a rich London wine merchant. It was just as she'd always known; George had never thought of her as a wife. But her sense of hurt was bitter all the same and she broke off their friendship.

She began to look more kindly on Mr Nicholls. And in January 1854, with her father's permission, she took to meeting him on the path – later known as 'Charlotte's Lane' – between Haworth and nearby Oxenhope, where he was staying. He renewed his suit. And finally, after Mr Brontë had come round to the idea, she accepted.

Years before, aged 19, Charlotte had claimed that she could only marry a man who she adored and would be willing to die for. Mr Nicholls was not such a man. She liked and respected him – 'He is always reliable, truthful, faithful, affectionate; a little unbending perhaps, but still persuadable' – without loving him.

'What I taste of happiness is of the soberest order. I trust to love my husband,' she wrote to Ellen, hardly sounding like an ecstatic bride-to-be.

But Mr Nicholls offered an escape from loneliness and her own gloomy thoughts. It might be her last chance.

The wedding, on June 29th, at 8am, was a quiet affair. Ellen Nussey and Miss Wooler, Charlotte's old headmistress, who had become a friend, (Charlotte described her as improving with age, like a good wine), were the only guests. Charlotte wore a simple, white muslin dress with green embroidery and a white bonnet trimmed with lace and flowers. The Haworth villagers said she looked like a snowdrop.

At the last minute Mr Brontë, pleading illness, announced he couldn't give Charlotte away. Probably he just couldn't bear to hand his daughter over to Mr Nicholls. Fortunately, Miss Wooler stepped in and saved the day.

The new Mr and Mrs Nicholls went to Ireland for their honeymoon, where Charlotte met her husband's relatives and found that she liked them and, more importantly, that she liked him. Afterwards they returned to Haworth, to the parsonage. Mr Nicholls took up his old curate's job and Charlotte continued to look after her father. She began to feel that marriage rather agreed with her and she grew fonder and fonder of Mr Nicholls, or 'dear Arthur', as she now called him.

'My own life is more occupied than it used to be. I have not so much time for thinking,' she told Ellen. Charlotte's health improved and she was happier than she had been for years. Her happiness would be short-lived.

One day in November 1854, Charlotte and Arthur walked out across the moors, to see a water-fall that Charlotte particularly loved. They were ambushed, without proper clothes, by a violent storm of rain and Charlotte caught a chill, which she then couldn't shake off. She also discovered that she was pregnant and the pregnancy made her horribly sick. By January she was confined to her bed. Arthur nursed her devotedly, but she seemed to be disappearing before his eyes. Martha Brown, the maid, remembered her as looking like a tiny bird, a 'throssel', in the big, mahogany four-poster, the same bed her mother had died in. She would open her mouth, like a beak, for morsels of food. Her transparent hand rested on the covers like a puff of thistledown.

In March she seemed a little better, but not for long. Howling gales battered the parsonage night and day and with them Charlotte herself seemed to blow away. On 31st March 1855, three weeks before her 39th birthday, she died and her baby died with her. She was buried in the family vault, along with her mother, brother and sisters.

Mr Nicholls and Mr Brontë, who had both loved Charlotte, lived on in the parsonage, side by side but rarely speaking to each other, for another six years, until Mr Brontë died also.

Key Dates

1816 – Charlotte is born in Thornton, Yorkshire.

1820 – The Brontë family move into the parsonage at Haworth.

1821 – Charlotte's mother dies.

1824 – Charlotte joins her elder sisters, Maria and Elizabeth, at the Clergy Daughters' School, Cowan Bridge.

1824 (9 months later) – Maria and Elizabeth die of consumption and Charlotte leaves Cowan Bridge and continues her education at home with her brother Branwell and sisters, Emily and Anne.

1831 – Charlotte is sent to another school, at Roe Head.

1832 – She returns to Haworth and teaches Emily and Anne.

1835 – She accepts a job, teaching at the Roe Head school.

1835 – She receives her first proposal of marriage and refuses.

1839 – She becomes a governess.

1842 – She and Emily go to Brussels to study French at the Pensionnat Heger and Charlotte falls in love with Monsieur Heger.

1843 – She returns to Yorkshire.

1846 – A volume of *Poems* is published, by Currer, Ellis and Acton Bell (alias Charlotte, Emily and Anne Brontë).

1847 – *Jane Eyre* is published by Currer Bell.
1848 – Charlotte and Anne go to London to reveal their identities to their publishers.

1848 (2 months later) – Branwell dies of consumption.

1848 (3 months later) – Emily dies of consumption.

1849 – Anne dies of consumption.

1852 – Arthur Nicholls, the curate at Haworth, proposes and Charlotte turns him down.

1854 – She agrees to marry Mr Nicholls.

1855 – Charlotte dies, pregnant with her first child.

Kate Hubbard is the author of *A Material Girl: Bess of Hardwick* (Short Books 2001), and *Charlotte Brontë, The Girl who Turned her Life into a Book*, another in the WHO WAS... children's biography series. She lives in London and Dorset.

Dear Reader,

No matter how old you are, good books always leave you wanting to know more. If you have any questions you would like to ask the author, **Kate Hubbard,** about **Charlotte Brontë** please write to us at: SHORT BOOKS 15 Highbury Terrace, London N5 1UP.

If you enjoyed this title, then you would probably enjoy others in the series. Why not click on our website for more information and see what the teachers are being told? **www.theshortbookco.com**

All the books in the WHO WAS... series are available from TBS, Distribution Centre, Colchester Road, Frating Green, Colchester, Essex CO7 7DW (Tel: 01206 255800), at £4.99 + P&P.

On the beach stood a wild thing waving its arms and hollering. The thing had the shape of a man, but it was all covered in fur, like a Barbary ape. What was it? A new kind of animal? A monster?

It was Alexander Selkirk, Scottish mariner and adventurer, thrilled to be rescued by passing sailors after four years alone on a Pacific island. This is the story of how Selkirk came to be stranded on the island and how he survived, the story of... THE REAL ROBINSON CRUSOE.

ISBN: 1-904095-79-8

WHO WAS... Queen Victoria
The Woman who Ruled the World
Kate Hubbard

Victoria was just 18 when she was crowned Queen in 1837 – a tiny figure with a will of iron. Never was there so queenly a queen. She made Britain great, and the people loved her for it.

In 1861 tragedy struck, when her husband Albert died. The little Queen loved dogs and cream cakes and the troops who fought her wars, but most of all she loved Albert. Dumb with grief, she hid herself away. Suddenly it seemed the woman who had made the monarchy so strong would destroy it. Could anyone persuade Victoria to be Queen again?

ISBN: 1-904095-82-8

Ned Kelly
Gangster hero of the Australian outback
Charlie Boxer
1-904095-61-5

William Shakespeare
The mystery of the world's greatest playwright
Rupert Christiansen
1-904095-81-X

Florence Nightingale
The lady with the lamp
Charlotte Moore
1-904095-83-6

Madame Tussaud
Waxwork queen of the French Revolution
Tony Thorne
1-904095-85-2

Nelson Mandela
The prisoner who became a President
Adrian Hadland
1-904095-86-0

The Bloody Baron
Evil invader of the East
Nick Middleton
1-904095-87-9

In case of difficulty in purchasing any Short Books
title through normal channels, please contact
BOOKPOST Tel: 01624 836000
Fax: 01624 837033
email: bookshop@enterprise.net
www.bookpost.co.uk
Please quote ref. 'Short Books'